Date: 12/7/16

Monkeys

Julie Murray

Abdo
I LIKE ANIMALS!
Kids

abdopublishing.com

Published by Abdo Kids, a division of ABDO, PO Box 398166, Minneapolis, Minnesota 55439.
Copyright © 2017 by Abdo Consulting Group, Inc. International copyrights reserved in all countries.
No part of this book may be reproduced in any form without written permission from the publisher.

Printed in the United States of America, North Mankato, Minnesota.

052016

092016

 THIS BOOK CONTAINS
RECYCLED MATERIALS

Photo Credits: iStock, Shutterstock

Production Contributors: Teddy Borth, Jennie Forsberg, Grace Hansen

Design Contributors: Candice Keimig, Dorothy Toth

Cataloging-in-Publication Data

Names: Murray, Julie, author.

Title: Monkeys / by Julie Murray.

Description: Minneapolis, MN : Abdo Kids, [2017] | Series: I like animals! |
    Includes bibliographical references and index.

Identifiers: LCCN 2015959204 | ISBN 9781680805338 (lib. bdg.) |
    ISBN 9781680805895 (ebook) | ISBN 9781680806458 (Read-to-me ebook)

Subjects: LCSH: Monkeys--Juvenile literature.

Classification: DDC 599.8--dc23

LC record available at http://lccn.loc.gov/2015959204

Table of Contents

Monkeys 4

Some Kinds
of Monkeys 22

Glossary. 23

Index 24

Abdo Kids Code. 24

Monkeys

Most monkeys live in trees.

Some live on the ground.

They have long arms.

Their legs are long, too.

These help them climb.

Monkeys have thumbs.

They hold things with them.

Some monkeys have long tails. Tails are for **balance**. They are also for hanging from trees!

Monkeys can be brown or gray. Some are reddish. Others have **bright** colors.

Monkeys eat leaves and fruit.

They also eat seeds and bark.

Some monkeys are big.

The mandrill is the biggest.

Some are small.

Marmosets are the smallest.

Do you like monkeys?

Some Kinds of Monkeys

common squirrel monkey

Japanese macaque

golden lion tamarin

white-faced saki

Glossary

balance
to keep from falling over.

bark
the tough covering of trees.

bright
very light and strong.

Index

arm 6

climb 6

color 12

food 14

ground 4

legs 6

mandrill 16

marmoset 18

size 16, 18

tail 10

thumb 8

tree 4, 10

abdokids.com

Use this code to log on to abdokids.com and access crafts, games, videos, and more!

Abdo Kids Code:
IMK5338